CW00427949

The Shaw Family History

FIDE · ET · FORTITUDINE

SHAW

By Charles Seaman

No part of this publication may be produced, stored in a retrieval
system or transmitted in any form or by any means electronic,
mechanical, photocopying, microfilming, recording or otherwise
without the prior permission of the author and The Aberdeen and
North East Scotland Family History Society.

Copyright The author and Aberdeen and North East Scotland Family History Society.
First published August 1999.

ISBN 1-900173-18-2

Published by:-
Aberdeen and North East Scotland Family History Society,
164 King Street, Aberdeen AB24 5BD

Printed By:-
Rainbow Enterprises, Howe Moss Crescent, Kirkhill Industrial Estate, Dyce, Aberdeen

ACKNOWLEDGEMENTS

The extracts from the Census Records and Old Parish Registers quoted throughout this work are reproduced by courtesy of the Registrar General of Scotland.

The postcard on page 29 shows St Nicholas Street leading to George Street in the late 1880s. It is ref. C1155 in the George Washington Wilson Collection, Aberdeen University Library, and is reproduced here with permission.

The death notices and obituaries quoted throughout this work are reproduced with thanks to the Press and Journal.

Introduction

I started looking into my wife's maternal grandmother's side of the family during 1994. I found it interesting and learnt a lot about the North East of Scotland while doing my research.

As in all family history investigations there is never an end and I have still a few leads to follow up.

My hope is people who read this might be able to help with information and send it to me at the address below.

I hope you enjoy reading this record of a family's history and find it interesting.

Charles Seaman
7 Kent Street,
Dunfermline,
Fife,
KY12 ODJ.

INDEX

	Page	Name	Ref. No.	Birth Date
Introduction				
Tree				
The Shaw Family	1	William Shaw	Ref. 625	
Second Generation				
	2	John Shaw	Ref. 185	02/11/1796
	10	Margaret Shaw	Ref. 1133	01/02/1807
Third Generation				
	11	Margaret Shaw	Ref. 187	24/08/1825
	13	William Shaw	Ref. 247	23/05/1829
	17	Elizabeth Shaw	Ref. 192	17/02/1840
	20	Mary Ann Shaw	Ref. 194	26/07/1842
	21	Helen Shaw	Ref. 195	17/06/1844
	22	George Shaw	Ref. 175	15/08/1846
	31	Catherine Sim	Ref. 1143	1847/48
Fourth Generation				
	33	John Strachan	Ref. 738	10/06/1859
	33	Isabella Ross	Ref. 647	03/05/1869
	34	William Ross	Ref. 219	26/11/1872
	34	Agnes Wilson	Ref. 713	25/10/1866
	35	Robert Shaw	Ref. 182	22/12/1898
	36	George Shaw	Ref. 183	22/12/1898
	37	Gwendoline A.W. Shaw	Ref. 155	04/04/1902
Fifth Generation				
	38	Moira Robertson	Ref. 716	
	38	Betty Shaw	Ref. 255	1944
	38	Josephine Shaw	Ref. 230	12/07/1947
	38	John Smiley	Ref. 157	17/10/1941
	40	Gwendoline Smiley	Ref. 156	11/05/1943
	42	Margaret Smiley	Ref. 150	05/07/1945
Sixth Generation				
	45	Sean Leroy	Ref. 227	
	45	Yvonne Leroy	Ref. 228	
	46	Elita Smiley	Ref. 237	09/12/1970
	46	Melanie Iliffe	Ref. 243	18/11/1966

** Note the list above shows the head of each family in context to the Shaw's. **

The Shaw Family Tree

Edward McCormack (718)

Megan Ann LeRoy (1290)

Sean Leroy (227)
m - Rebecca

Yvonne LeRoy (228)
m - Mr Lee

Philip Lee (1292)

Robbie Moir (232)

Lucy Moir (233)

Hamish Moir (234)

Peter J. Storey (1120)

Philip G. Smiley (236)
m - Yvonne Turley

Elita Smiley (237)
m - Mark Storey

Michael Storey (1294)

Nicholas Smiley (238)
m - Christina Lundy

Laura Smiley (239)

Alexander H. Smiley (240)

Simon P. Smiley (241)

Amanda R. Nitychoruk (256)

Melanie Iliffe (243)
m - Adam Nitychoruk

Joseph M. Nitychoruk (257)

Luke Nitychoruk (1180)

Roger Iliffe (244)
m - Ildiko Maczko

Tracy Jane Iliffe (245)

Emma Rose Iliffe (246)
m - Robert Lee

David A. Bowie (151)
m - Laura Dunlop

Fiona M. Bowie (2)
m - Charles G. Seaman

Euan A. Bowie (152)

William Strachan (735)

Elizabeth Strachan (736)

Mary Ann Strachan (737)
m - George Bennett

John Strachan (738)
m - Annie Morrison

Patrick Strachan (739)

Mary A. Strachan (751)

Elsie M. Strachan (752)

William A. Webster (650)

James G. Webster (651)

Ann Shaw (1136)

Isabella Shaw (250)

William Shaw (1135)

George Paul Shaw (249)

Isobel M. Ross (220)
m - Farquhar McRitchie

Elizabeth Ross (645)
m - William Draine

Mary Ann Ross (646)

Isabella Ross (647)
m - James L. Webster

William Ross (219)
m - Isabella R. Greig

Moira Robertson (716)
m - Mr McCormick

John A. Wilson (712)

Agnes Wilson (713)
m - Robert C. Robertson

Mary A. Wilson (714)

Robert John Shaw (224)

Betty Shaw (225)
m - Philip LeRoy

John Wright (691)

William Wright (719)

James A.G. Wright (720)

George Wright (721)

Peter Wright (722)

Josephine Shaw (230)
m - Len Moir

Nellie Shaw (1st Wife) (177)

John Shaw (179)

Cecilia Shaw (180)

Josephine Shaw (181)

Robert Shaw (182)
m - Helen

George Shaw (183)
m - May Watt

Alice A.Y. Shaw (184)

Mary Ann Smiley (158)

John Smiley (157)
m - Anita Coletti

Gwendoline Smiley (156)
m - Gerald Iliffe

Margaret Smiley (150)
m - David Bowie

Gwendoline A.W. Shaw (155)
m - Hugh Smiley

Margaret Shaw (187)
m - William Strachan

Isabel Shaw (814)

William Shaw (247)
m - Eliza Bennett

Jannet Shaw (188)

John Shaw (189)

Alexander Shaw (190)

James Shaw (191)

Elizabeth Shaw (192)
m - James Ross

Mary Ann Shaw (194)
m - William Wilson

Helen Shaw (195)
m - Peter Wright

George Shaw (175)
m - Margaret Tawse
m - Christina Youngson

Margaret S. Jack (1144)

Lizzie Jack (1181)

Thomas W. Jack (1145)

Catherine Jack (1182)

Henry Jack (1183)

William Shaw (625)
m - Margaret Steinson

John Shaw (185)
m - Mary Green

Isobel Shaw (1130)

Catherine Shaw (1131)

William Shaw (1132)

Margaret Shaw (1133)
m - James Sim

Jannet Shaw (1134)

Catherine Sim (1143)
m - John Jack

The Shaw Family

This is the family which starts with William Shaw who was a mason and was married to Margaret Steinson.

1.   William Shaw, Ref. 625,
      Occ.- Mason.
      Married - 24/01/1796, Keith, Banffshire
      Spouse - Margaret Steinson, Ref. 626,

Old Parish Records for Keith 23/01/1796
William Shaw & Margaret Steinson both in this parrish were matrimonially contracted after publication of bands were married the 24th.

      Children:

            i   John Shaw, Ref. 185,(See No. 2)
                   Born - 02/11/1796

            ii   Isabella Shaw, Ref. 1130,
                   Born - 01/11/1800, Newmill, Keith, Banffshire.
                   Baptised - 06/11/1800, Keith, Banffshire.
                   Died - 13/03/1874, Old Machar Poorhouse, Aberdeen.
                   Occ.- Domestic Servant.

Old Parish Records for Keith 06/11/1800
Isobel lawful daughter to William Shaw and Margaret Steinson in Newhill was born the 1st Nov and baptised this day. Witnesses - Mr John Morison and Isobel Allan in Newhill.

            iii   Catherine Shaw, Ref. 1131,
                   Born - 28/06/1803, Clerkseat, Grange, Banffshire.
                   Baptised - 28/06/1803, Grange, Banffshire.

Old Parish Records for Grange 28/06/1803
William Shaw in Clerk Seat had a child by his wife Margt. Stivenson baptised and called Cathcrine. - Witnesses - John Bannerman and Catherine Shaw.

            iv   William Shaw, Ref. 1132,
                   Born - 26/03/1805, Grange, Banffshire.
                   Baptised - 26/03/1805, Grange, Banffshire.

Old Parish Records for Grange 26/03/1805
William Shaw in Clerk Seat had a child by his wife Margaret Stevenson baptised and called William. Witnesses - William Bannerman and Janet Godsman.

            v   Margaret Shaw, Ref. 1133, (See No. 3)
                   Born - 01/02/1807

vi   Jannet Shaw, Ref. 1134,
            Born - 06/09/1809, Clgahrat, Grange, Banffshire.
            Baptised - 06/09/1809, Clgahrat, Grange, Banffshire.

Old Parish Records for Grange 09/06/1809

William Shaw in Clgahrat had a daughter by his wife Margt. Steinson baptised and named Jannet. Witnesses - John Baniman, Clgahrat & Janet Bain, Archiston.

SECOND GENERATION

2.   John Shaw, Ref. 185,
           Born - 02/11/1796, Newmill, Keith, Banffshire.
           Baptised - 04/11/1796, Keith, Banffshire
           Died - 29/11/1883, Bellhangie, Birse
           Buried - Allenvale Cemetery, Aberdeen.
           Occ.- Miller & Crofter(3 acres at Hillcroft, Fordyce),
           Married - 21/11/1824, Preshome R.C. Church, Banffshire
           Spouse - Mary Green, Ref. 186,
                    (Daughter of John Green & Janet Reid)
           Born - 15/09/1803, Enzie, Banffshire,
           Died - 24/09/1887, 22 Bridge Street, Aberdeen.
           Buried - 27/09/1887, Allenvale Cemetery, Aberdeen.

Old Parish Records for Keith 03/11/1796

John lawful son to William Shaw and Margaret Steinson in Newmill was born 2nd Curr. and baptised 4th inst. Witnesses - John Gordon at Vaunit Cairn & Miss Isobel Chalmers in Newhill.

The two records below show that John and Mary were of two different religions or there was a problem at the time being married in the Catholic church so had to be married in Church of Scotland to make it legal.

Old Parish Records for Rathven 05/12/1824

John Shaw & Mary Green both in this parish were matrimonially contracted and after publication of bands were Married.

Preshome Catholic Records 21/11/1824

John Shaw (Prot.) at Mill of Buckie & Mary Green near the cove having been proclaimed & no impediment having appeared were married in presence of John Green, Alex Bennet & others by me Alex Badenoch.

      Children :
               i   Margaret Shaw, Ref. 187 (See No.4)
                     Born - 24/08/1825,

               ii   Isabel Shaw, Ref. 814
                     Born - 01/08/1827, Mill of Buckie, Banffshire

Baptised - 01/08/1827, Preshome R.C. Church, Banffshire
Died - 23/05/1828, Mill of Buckie, Banffshire

Preshome Catholic Records 1/8/1827
In the same day I baptised Isobel lawful daughter of John Shaw & Mary Green, Mill of Buckie. Isabel Ogilvie and John Benzies stood sponsor.

iii   William Shaw, Ref. 247 (See No.5)
Born - 23/05/1829,

iv   Jannet Shaw, Ref. 188,
Born - 27/07/1831, Gallochy, Banffshire
Baptised - 29/07/1831, Preshome R.C. Church, Banffshire.
Died - 22/12/1856, Moss Street, Keith
Buried - Burying Ground of Keith

Preshome Catholic Records 29/07/1831
Jannet Lawful daughter of John Shaw & Mary Green born at Gallochy on the 27th July 1831 and was baptised by me on the 29 day of the same month. The sponsors were Alexander Smith & Jannet Reid.

Jannet died age 24 of Scarlet Fever according to the death certificate.

v   John Shaw, Ref. 189,
Born - 15/08/1833, Mill of Buckie, Banffshire,
Baptised - 16/08/1833, Preshome R.C. Church, Banffshire.
Died - 19/07/1900, 51 Stanley Street, Aberdeen,
Buried - 24/07/1900, Snow Churchyard, Aberdeen,
Occ.- Priest.

Preshome Catholic Records 16/08/1833
John Lawful son of John Shaw & Mary Green born on the 15 August 1833 was baptised by me on this 16 Aug. 1833. The sponsors were Jannet Green & John Simpson.

Aberdeen Journal 21/07/1900
Deaths - Shaw - At 51 Stanley Street, Aberdeen, on the 19th inst. Rev. John Shaw, R.C. Clergyman, Age 65 R.I.P.

Aberdeen Journal 22/07/1900
Public Notices - The Funeral of the Late Rev. John Shaw will take place on Tuesday 24th curt. from St. Mary's Cathedral, Huntly Street to The Snow Churchyard. The funeral service will commence at 11am and at the conclusion the cortège will leave for the cemetery. All friends respectfully invited to attend.

FUNERAL OF REV. JOHN SHAW, ABERDEEN
AN IMPRESSIVE CEREMONY

The funeral of the late Rev. John Shaw took place yesterday from St. Mary's Cathedral, Huntly

Street, to the Snow Churchyard, Old Aberdeen. The funeral service, which commenced at eleven o'clock, consisted of a Pontifical High Mass of Requiem, Right Rev. E.Chisholm, LL.D., Bishop of Aberdeen, officiating, assisted by Rev. George Shaw, St. Mary's Cathedral, nephew of deceased deacon and Rev. Joseph Mclellan, Stonehaven - sub deacon. Amongst the other clergy present were - Right Rev. Monsignor Fraser, rector, Scots College, Rome; Right Rev. Monsignor Techetti, Aberdeen; Right Rev. Monsignor Clapperton, St. Andrew's, Dundee; Rev. Canon Clapperton, Buckie; Rev. Canon MacDonald, Inverurie; Rev. James McGregor, rector, St. Mary's College, Blairs; and Rev. Professors McBain, Miley, Walsh and McHardy; Rev. J.C. Meany, administrator, St. Mary's Cathedral, and Rev. Andrew Grant; Rev. Vincent MacDonald, Arbroath; REV. Mr McInnes, Paisley; Rev. Thos. Macdonald, St. Peter's, Aberdeen; Rev. Chas. Devine, St. Joseph's, Woodside; Rev. George Wiseman, Fraserburgh; and Rev. Joseph Thomson, Aboyne. The catafalque was placed in the sanctuary in front of the high alter and the service of the mass was chanted by all the clergy present, led by the chanters--Rev. Professor Miley and Rev. Joseph Thomson. Suitable music was also rendered by the choir, under Mr J.Keenan, Miss Taylor presiding at the organ. The service throughout was of a most impressive nature and Rev. Andrew Grant was master of ceremonies. Besides the relatives of deceased and other mourners there was present a large number of the general public. The children of Nazareth House were accommodated with seats in one of the aisles. Taking for his text the words - "Blessed are those servants whom the Lord when He cometh shall find watching. Be you then also ready"-Luke xii., 37 and 40. Rev. J.C. Meany delivered an eloquent funeral oration, in which he said that all who knew Father John Shaw united in saying that his life was singulary unobtrusive. That is the world's way of expressing that "his life was hidden with Christ in God." Like so many other men chosen by God to take part in the revival of Catholicism in Scotland, Father Shaw came from the Enzie, whose glory it was to have always kept the faith and to have been stronghold and the nursery of the faith. He was born there some 66 years ago. At the age of eleven he was sent to Ratisbon, the college of the Scot's Benedictines. There he spent the whole of his course of ecclesiastical study. In the year 1858 he returned to Scotland, and was ordained at Preshome. He spent the first year of his missionary life at Preshome and Tynett. Thence he was sent to Ballogie on Deeside. While at Ballogie he served the station of

(Picture on this page is of the gravestone in Snow churchyard)

4

Dee Castle, but as Catholics had begun to gather in the rising village of Aboyne, Father Shaw undertook to build there a church and presbytery. The present Catholic church and adjoining house at Aboyne are a monument to his zeal. Between Ballogie and Aboyne Father Shaw spent a period of 17 years. He was transferred in 1875 to Belechin in Perthshire and during the course of his nine years ministry he succeeded in erecting a church in Aberfeldy. He was afterwards stationed at Montrose, where the present Catholic church owes its existence to him, and he bought the old Anglican church at Brechin for the Catholic congregation there. Failing health compelled him to seek a life of less activity, and he was appointed by Archbishop Smith chaplain to the Little Sisters of the Poor in Edinburgh. Here Father Shaw laboured for 12 years. Only last summer, when bodily ailments made rest imperative, he retired from missionary life , and took up his home in Aberdeen. His life showed a record of work of which any priest might well be proud. Nevertheless, in the midst of it all, his motto might well have been the words of St. John the Baptist - "He must increase, but I must decrease"; or those other words in the Imitation of Christ- "Love to be unknown and to be despised." Father Meany (continuing) said that during the last few weeks, when it was privilege to stand and minister at the bedside of Father Shaw, some words of Scripture came continually into his mind. These were the words of Balam's blessing to King Balac words of praise to the holy dead of Israel "Let my soul die the death of the just, and my last end be like to them"(Numbers xxiii. 10). Father Meany concluded by paying a gracefully worded tribute to the virtues of the deceased. After the conclusion of the service the coffin was borne from the cathedral by members of Shore Porters' Society, the organ pealing forth Chopin's Funeral March. The Cathedral bell was tolled at intervals. The cortège, which left the cathedral shortly after twelve o'clock, included the clergy and a large number of personal friends of deceased. Rev. George Shaw conducted the service at the churchyard.

Extract from The Catholic Directory 1901

OBITUARY

Pray for the repose of the soul of the Rev. John Shaw, who died at Aberdeen on the 20th July, 1900, in the 67th year of his age and the 42nd of his priesthood.
The main features of Fr. Shaw's life were eloquently set forth in the discourse which the Rev. John C. Meany, Aberdeen, delivered at his funeral, and of which we give here a short resume. Preaching from St. Luke, xii. 37 Fr. Meany said: All who knew Fr. John Shaw would unite in saying that his life was singularly unobtrusive. That is the world's way of expressing what must in some degree be true of every priest, that " his life was hidden with Christ in God". Like so many other men chosen by God to take part in the revival of Catholicism in Scotland, Fr. Shaw came from the Enzie, whose glory it was to have always kept the faith, to have been the stronghold and the nursery of the faith. He was born there on the 15th August, 1833, and at the age of eleven he was sent to Ratisbon, the college of the Scot's Benedictines. There he spent the whole of his course of ecclesiastical study. In the year 1858 he returned to Scotland, and was ordained at Preshome. He spent the first year of his missionary life at Preshome and Tynett. Thence he was sent to Ballogie on Deeside. While at Ballogie he served the station of Dee Castle, but as Catholics had begun to gather in the rising village of Aboyne, Father Shaw undertook to build there a church and presbytery. The present Catholic church and adjoining house at Aboyne are a monument to his zeal. Between Ballogie and Aboyne Father Shaw spent a period of 17 years. He was transferred in 1875 to Belechin in Perthshire and during the course of his nine years ministry he succeeded in erecting a church in Aberfeldy. He was afterwards stationed at Montrose, where the present Catholic church owes its

existence to him, and he bought the old Anglican church at Brechin for the Catholic congregation there. Failing health compelled him to seek a life of less activity, and he was appointed by Archbishop Smith chaplain to the Little Sisters of the Poor in Edinburgh. Here Father Shaw laboured for 12 years. Only last summer, when bodily ailments made rest imperative, he retired from missionary life , and took up his home in Aberdeen. His life showed a record of work of which any priest might well be proud. Nevertheless, in the midst of it all, his motto might well have been the words of St. John the Baptist - "He must increase, but I must decrease"; or those other words in the Imitation of Christ- "Love to be unknown and to be despised." Fr. Meany referred in touching terms to the last few weeks of Fr. Shaw's life, and said that often for hours without intermission he suffered the most heart-piercing pain; but though his frame heaved and his face was convulsed, his lips moved in words of patience or his hands struggled to make the sign of the Cross. He bemoaned the bodily weakness which prevented him from reciting his habitual prayers, but he would take up his crucifix and kiss it fervently. It was suggested to him that he should thank God for the work he had been able to accomplish in his sacred ministry, and his reply was: "Oh, don't speak of it:it is nothing". Every day when he said Mass he looked with eyes of faith beyond the bourne of time to the sojourn of the just who are in the hands of God, to the home of the souls whose exile is prolonged, and he besought for them a place of refreshment, light and peace. Now, from his own exile his voice called to them:"My soul hath thirsted after Thee, the strong and living God, when shall I come and appear before Thy face?"

The funeral service was held on the 24th July at the Cathedral, Aberdeen. Bishop Chisolm was celebrant, Rev.John C. Meany assistant priest, the Rev. George P. Shaw and Joseph Mclennan deacon and sub-deacon and the Rev. Andrew Grant master of ceremonies. A body of clergy rendered the plain chant of the service. After the Absolutions had been pronounced by the Bishop the remains were conveyed to the Snow Churchyard, at Old Aberdeen. Fr. George Shaw, a nephew of the deceased, pronounced the last prayers at the grave.

(Pictured above is Aboyne RC church in 1995)

1861 Census Petarch, Birse, Aberdeenshire

Name	C	S	A	Occupation	Birth Place
Rev. John Shaw	H	U	27	Roman Catholic Clergyman	Banffshire/ Rathven
Elizabeth Shaw	Si	U	21	House Keeper	Banffshire/ Fordyce

1871 Census Tillenbach Catholic Chapel, Birse, Aberdeenshire

Name	C	S	A	Occupation	Birth Place
Rev. John Shaw	H	U	37	Catholic Clergyman	Banffshire/ Rathven
Isabella Green	Au	U	61	General Ser.	Banffshire/ Rathven
Charles Moir	Se	U	10	Scholar	Aberdeenshire/ Birse

Left is a picture of the house which I think was Tillenbach Catholic Chapel at Birse, Aberdeenshire in the 1870's.

vi   Alexander Shaw, Ref. 190,
Born - 17/10/1835, Towie Parish, Banffshire
Occ - Miller
Died - 09/08/1857, Den Mill, Parish of Tough, Aberdeenshire
Buried - Parish Churchyard of Tough

Death Certificate
Alexander's death certificate says he died of accidental drowning while bathing in a mill dam. He was under water about an hour and a half.

Keith Catholic Records 16/08/1857
SHAW - Drowned whilst bathing on the Sunday forenoon during mass, Alexander Shaw died aged 20.

vii   James Shaw, Ref. 191,
Born - 22/10/1837, Towie Parish, Banffshire

viii   Elizabeth Shaw, Ref. 192 (See No.6),
Born - 17/02/1840,

7

ix   Mary Ann Shaw, Ref. 194 (See No.7)
Born - 26/07/1842,

xi   Helen Shaw, Ref. 195 (See No.8)
Born - 17/06/1844,

xii   George Shaw, Ref.175 (See No.9),
Born - 15/08/1846,

Picture on the left is of Mill of Buckie farm as it stands in Oct 1996. The mill is a ruin with just a small part of wall left.

Picture on the left is of Mill of Towie, Fordyce, Banff-shire where John Shaw and family lived in the 1840's and the adjacent Mill Croft where they stayed in the 1850's.

On the next page there are Census records between 1840 & 1881 involving John Shaw & Family.

1841 Census, Millerd of Towie, Fordyce, Banffshire

Name	Age	Occupation	Birth
John Shaw	40	Miller	Y
Mary Shaw	30		Y
Margaret Shaw	14		Y
Janet Shaw	9		Y
John Shaw	7		Y
Alex Shaw	5		Y
James Shaw	3		Y
Elspet Shaw	1		Y
Euphemia Smith	2m		Y

1851 Census Millcroft, Fordyce, Banffshire

Name	C	S	A	Occupation	Birth Place
John Shaw	H	M	57	Miller & Crofter	Banffshire/ Keith
Mary Shaw	W	M	47		Banffshire/ Bellie
John Shaw	S	U	17	Scholar	Banffshire/ Rathven
Alexander Shaw	S	U	15	Scholar	Banffshire/ Fordyce
James Shaw	S		13	Scholar	Banffshire/ Fordyce
Alice Shaw	D		10	Scholar	Banffshire/ Fordyce
Mary Ann Shaw	D		8	Scholar	Banffshire/ Fordyce
Helen Shaw	D		6	Scholar	Banffshire/ Fordyce
George Shaw	S		4	Scholar	Banffshire/ Fordyce

I think Alice is a mistake and should read Elizabeth or Elspeth as Alice doesn't appear in the family Bible along with all the other children.

1861 Census Moss Street, Keith, Banffshire

Name	C	S	A	Occupation	Birth Place
Mary Shaw	H	M	58	Inn Keepers Wife	Banffshire/ Rathven
Mary Ann Shaw	D	U	19	Inn Keepers Waiter	Banffshire/ Fordyce
Helen Shaw	D	U	17	Inn Keepers Waiter	Banffshire/ Fordyce
George Shaw	S		14	Drapers Apprentice	Banffshire/ Fordyce
James McLachlan Shaw	GS		4		Banffshire/ Kieth

1881 Census Ballhangie, Birse, Aberdeenshire

Name	C	S	A	Occupation	Birth Place
John Shaw	H	M	84	Formerly Meal Miller	Banffshire/ Fordyce
Mary Shaw	W	M	78		Banffshire/ Fordyce

Picture on left is of Bellhangie Cottage as it stands in 1995. John Shaw and his wife lived in it during early 1880's.

3. Margaret Shaw, Ref. 1133,
    Born - 01/02/1807, Grange, Banffshire
    Baptised - 01/02/1807, Grange, Banffshire
    Died - 17/04/1897, 31 Hutcheon Street, Aberdeen
    Married - 06/05/1842, Old Machar parish, Aberdeen,
    Spouse - James Sim, Ref. 1142,
    Occ.- Gardener

Old Parish Records for Grange 01/02/1807
William Shaw had a child by his wife Margaret Steinson baptised and called Margaret. Witnesses -
James McDonald and Margaret Dustan.

Children:
        i   Catherine Sim, Ref. 1143 (See No. 10)
                 Born - 1847/48 Approx,

THIRD GENERATION

4.   Margaret Shaw, Ref. 187,
        Born - 24/08/1825, Mill of Buckie, Enzie, Banffshire
        Died - 22/11/1911. Lintmill, King Edward, Aberdeenshire
        Married - 22/03/1851, Marnoch, Banffshire,
        Spouse - William Strachan, Ref. 734,
              (Son of John Strachan & Elizabeth Paterson)
        Born - 1826 Approx, Turriff, Aberdeenshire,
        Died - 14/03/1903, Morlass, King Edward, Aberdeenshire
        Occ.- Farmer

Preshome Catholic Records 26/08/1825
This 26th day of August eighteen hundred, twenty five years, I baptised Margaret lawful daughter of
John Shaw, miller at Buckie a protesta, and Mary Green his spouse. The sponsors were Alex
Bennett, Mill of Buckie and Margaret Forbes.

Children:
        i   William Strachan, Ref. 735,
                 Born - 15/02/1852, Mains of Birkinbeg, Fordyce, Banffshire,
                 Bap.- 21/02/1852, Mains of Birkinbeg, Fordyce, Banffshire,

Old Parish Records for Fordyce 21/02/1852
William, Lawful Son of Wm. Strachan at Mains of Birkinbeg & Margaret Shaw his wife, Born 15
Feb. 1852 & Baptised 21 Feb. 1852. Witnesses- Wm. Strachan, Farmer, Graymills & Ths. Davidson,
Moor of Glasshaiy.

        ii   Elizabeth Strachan, Ref. 736,
                 Bap.- 09/07/1853, Marnoch, Banffshire,

        iii   Mary Ann Strachan, Ref. 737,
                 Born - 25/12/1855, Knowhead of Crombie, Marnoch, Banffshire,
                 Married - 19/05/1887, Moreless, King Edward, Aberdeenshire,
                 Spouse - George Bennett, Ref. 745,
                     (Son of John Bennett & Catherine Scott)
                 Born - 1855 Approx,
                 Occ.- Waiter

iv   John Strachan, Ref. 738, (See No. 11)
Born - 10/06/1859,

v   Patrick Strachan, Ref. 739,
Born - 17/12/1862, Fordyce, Banffshire

There are two entries recording Margaret Shaw and William Strachan's wedding in OPR's.

Old Parish Records for Fordyce 01/03/1851
William Strachan in the Parish Marnoch and Margaret Shaw in this parish now matrimonially contracted March 1st & were afterwards married.

Old Parish Records for Marnoch 22/03/1851
M111614 0601 (I haven't seen the film yet.)

The Census records below are for the Strachan family for the years 1861,1881 & 1891.

1861 Census Craigmills, Fordyce, Banffshire.

Name	C	S	A	Occupation	Birth Place
Margaret Strachan	H	M	36	Farmer Overseer's Wife	Rathven, Banffshire
William Strachan	S		9	Scholar	Fordyce, Banffshire
Mary Ann Strachan	D		5		Marnoch, Banffshire
John Strachan	S		1		Fordyce, Banffshire

1881 Census Morlass, King Edward, Aberdeenshire.

Name	C	S	A	Occupation	Birth Place
William Strachan	H	M	54	Farmer of 105 acres.	Turriff, Aberdeenshire
Margaret Strachan	W	M	54	Farmers Wife	Rathven, Banffshire
John Strachan	S	U	20	Farmers Son	Fordyce, Banffshire
Patrick Strachan	S	U	18	Farmers Son	Fordyce, Banffshire
David Kennedy	Se	W	46	Farm Servant	King Edward, Aberdeenshire

1891 Census Morlass, King Edward, Aberdeenshire

Name	C	S	A	Occupation	Birth Place
William Strachan	H	M	64	Farmer	Turriff, Aberdeenshire
Margaret Strachan	W	M	64	Farmers Wife	Rathven, Banffshire
Ellen J. Milne	Se	U	17	Gen. Servant	King Edward, Aberdeenshire
George Wilson	Se	U	18	Farm Servant	Marnoch, Banffshire
Innes Philip	Se	U	16	Farm Servant	Mourquitter, Aberdeenshire
James Shearer	Se	U	14	Farm Servant	Turriff, Aberdeenshire

The Story of a Parish by James Godsman - King Edward

page 119-122 Moreless. 105 Acres   (extract from page 121)

Mr Wood, who was assisted in the management of the farm by his son, James, was succeeded in 1866 by William Strachan of the Montcoffer family. A new barn, its date stone reads 1888, was built during the tenancy of Mr Strachan, and a horse mill established. The water mill, which stood to the north, and slightly west of the avenue, fell into disuse, its final disappearance occured in 1925, when Mr Davidson took over the tenancy. Mr Strachan was succeededby his son John, who gave up the tenancy in 1906, and retired to the Lintmill of Strocherie.

5.   William Shaw, Ref. 247,
        Born - 23/05/1829, Mill of Buckie, Banffshire
        Baptised - 24/05/1829, Preshome R.C. Church, Banffshire.
        Occ - Out Fitter/Tailor
        Married - 30/06/1870, in the RC Church, Huntly St, Aberdeen.
        Spouse - Eliza Bennett, Ref. 248,
                (Daughter of John Bennett & Catherine Scott)
        Born - 11/05/1833, Birkenbush, Banffshire.
        Baptised - 12/05/1833, Preshome R.C. Church, Banffshire.
        Occ - Domestic Servant

        Children:
                i   Ann Shaw, Ref. 1135,
                        Born - 09/09/1871, 7 Nelson Street, Aberdeen

                ii   Isabella Shaw, Ref. 250,
                        Born - 16/10/1872, 7 Nelson Street, Aberdeen.
                        Occ.- Nun.

iii   William Shaw, Ref. 1136,
          Born - 09/07/1874, 7 Nelson Street, Aberdeen

iv   George Paul Shaw, Ref. 249,
          Born - 06/06/1876, 10 Cumon Place, Aberdeen
          Died - 01/04/1938, Blairs College, Aberdeen.
          Buried - 04/04/1938, Tomintoul,
          Educated - Blairs College, Aberdeen, (1889-1893)
          Occ.- Canon.

George wrote a book called An Old Story of a Highland Parish, published in 1926 by Sands & Co. costing 5/-. The book is available to read in Aberdeen Public Library Ref. No. X123 754 436 1230.

Pictured left is Canon George Paul Shaw and his housekeeper in Dufftown.

Valladolid 1893-99
Ordained Valladolid 1899
Lent to Shieldmuir 1899
Aberdeen Cathedral 1899-1905
Dufftown 1905-30
Tomintoul 1930-34
St. Mary's, Inverness 1934-38

Ref.- Scottish Secular Clergy 1879-1989.

The Aberdeen Press & Journal, Sat 2nd April 1938 Deaths.
Shaw - At Blairs College on 1st April 1938, the very Rev. Canon George P. Shaw, of the Catholic church, Inverness, age 61 years R.I.P. Pontifical Requiem Mass at Tomintoul, on Monday 4th inst. at 12 noon, and funeral there after.

The Aberdeen Press & Journal, Sat 2nd April 1938 Pg.8

Canon Shaw Dead
DEVOTEDLY SERVED R.C. CHURCH
HELD CHARGES IN NORTH
FATAL ILLNESS AT BLAIRS COLLEGE

The Very Rev. Canon George Paul Shaw, of the Roman Catholic Church, Inverness died yesterday at Blairs College at the age of sixty-one.

He had been in ill-health for several months.

Born in Aberdeen, Cannon Shaw entered Blairs College in 1889, and then went to the Scots College at Valladolid, Spain in 1893. He was ordained priest in Spain in 1899, and returning to this country was curate at St. Mary's Cathedral, Aberdeen, where he remained from 1899 to 1905, when he went to Dufftown. He was there until 1930. Canon Shaw in that year went to Tomintoul, and remained there until 1934, after which he went to Inverness. He was made a Canon of the Chapter in 1933. Canon Shaw gave a lifetime of devoted service to the Roman Catholic Church, and was highly esteemed.

The Aberdeen Press & Journal, April 5th 1938 Pg.3

LATE CANON SHAW
FUNERAL SERVICE AT TOMINTOUL

The funeral of Canon George Paul Shaw, of the Roman Catholic Church, Inverness, took place yesterday at Tomintoul where he was in service for a number of years before going to Inverness.

Pontifical Requiem Mass was conducted by the Right Rev. Bishop G.H. Bennett, Aberdeen, assisted by Mgr. Paterson, Aberdeen; Deacon Father M'Laughlan, Kelso; and Sub-Deacon Father Lewis M'William, Forres.

Mr Geo. Shaw, Aberdeen, a second cousin of Father Shaw and canons of the Roman Catholic Church acted as pall-bearers.

A memorial service to Canon G.P. Shaw was held at St. Mary's Chapel, Inverness. The service took the form of Requiem Mass sung by the children of St. Joseph's School. It was conducted by Father Gordon. In the course of an eloquent tribute to the Canon, who was parish priest at Inverness for four year, Father Gordon said that Canon Shaw devoted his whole life to the service of the church. His work in Inverness would be remembered particulary because he established a branch of the St Vincent de Paul Society and a branch of the Catholic Young Men's Society. His work on behalf of education would also be remembered throughout the whole of Inverness-shire.

<u>Extract from The Catholic Directory 1939 Obituary</u>

Pray for the soul of the VERY REV. GEORGE PAUL CANON SHAW who died on the 1st April in the 62nd year of his age and the 39th of his priesthood.

   The Very Rev. George Paul Canon Shaw was born at Aberdeen on the 18th June 1876. Entering Blairs College in 1889 he went to the Scot's College, Valladolid four years later and was ordained priest there on the 21st April, 1899. On his return to Scotland he was stationed for a short time at Shieldmuir and later at the Cathedral, Aberdeen. In 1905 he was appointed parish priest of Dufftown where he remained until 1930 when he was transferred to Tomintoul. In 1933 he was appointed to Inverness where he will always remembered for his zeal for souls and his great interest in the young people of the parish. He was in delicate health for the last year of his life and died at Blairs College. At his own request he was buried in Tomintoul. Solemn Requiem Mass was celebrated by the Bishop of Aberdeen. R.I.P.

<u>Preshome Catholic Records 24/05/1829</u>
William lawful son of John Shaw & Mary Green Born 23 May 1829 is baptised by me on this 24 May 1829. The sponsors were James Green and Janet Green.

<u>Preshome Catholic Records 12/05/1833</u>
Elizabeth lawful daughter of John Bennett & Catherine Scott born at Birkenbush on the 11 May 1833 was baptised by me on this 12 May 1833. The sponsors were William Scott & Catherine Bennett.

Below are the census records for 1841, 1881 & 1891 William Shaw & Family.

1841 Census Village of Fordyce, Fordyce

Name	A	Occupation	Birth Place
John Russell	60	Tailor	N
Janet Russell	50		Y
Frances Russell	20		Y
Leslie Russell	10		N
Wm Shaw	10	Tailor Apprentice	Y
Charles Guibron	15	Blksmith App.	Y

1881 Census 173 North Broadford, Aberdeen

Name	C	S	A	Occupation	Birth Place
William Shaw	H	M	51	Tailor Journeyman	Banffshire
Eliza Bennett	W	M	45		Banffshire
Isabella Shaw	D		8	Scholar	Aberdeenshire
George Shaw	S		4		Aberdeenshire
George Bennett	Bo	U	25	Grocers Assistant	Banffshire/ Elgin

Bo - Boarder

1891 Census 20 Hill Street, Aberdeen

Name	C	S	A	Occupation	Birth Place
William Shaw	H	M	62	Tailor	Banffshire, Enzie
El__? Shaw	W	M	53		Banffshire, Enzie
Bella Shaw	D	U	18		Aberdeenshire, Aberdeen

6.   Elisabeth Shaw, Ref. 192,
     Born - 17/02/1840, Towie Parish, Banffshire
     Married - 18/11/1862, Keith, Banffshire
     Spouse - James Ross, Ref. 221,
          (Son of Alexander Ross & Elizabeth Durwood)
     Baptised - 17/04/1820, Birse Parish Church, Aberdeenshire
     Occ. - Farmer

     Children :

          i   Elizabeth Ross, Ref. 645,
               Born - 11/11/1863, Tillinteach, Birse,
               Married - 16/03/1893, Tillinteach, Birse,
               Spouse - William Drainic, Ref. 648,
                    (Son of Alexander Drainie & Ann Rutherford)
               Born - 1862 Approx,
               Occ. - Carpenter

          ii   Mary Ann Ross, Ref. 646,
               Born - 28/01/1866, Tillinteach, Birse

          iii   Isabella Ross, Ref. 647(See No.12)
               Born - 03/05/1869

iv   William Ross, Ref. 219 (See No.13),
Born - 26/11/1872

Below are census records for James Ross and family starting in 1871.

1871 Census, Farm of Tillentiach, Birse, Aberdeenshire.

Name	C	S	A	Occupation	Birth Place
James Ross	H	M	50	Farmer of 120 acres	Aberdeenshire/ Birse
Elizabeth Ross	W	M	30		Banffshire/ Fordyce
Elizabeth Ross	D		7	Scholar	Aberdeenshire/ Birse
Mary Ann Ross	D		5	Scholar	Aberdeenshire/ Birse
Isabella Ross	D		1		Aberdeenshire/ Birse
Peter Stephen	Se	U	23	Farm Servant	Aberdeenshire/ Turriff
Elizabeth Aitken	Se	U	17	Domestic Ser.	Kincardine/ Strachan
George Aitken	Se	U	13	Farm Servant	Kincardine/ Strachan

1881 Census, Tillenteach, Birse, Aberdeenshire.

Name	C	S	A	Occupation	Birth Place
James Ross	H	M	61	Farmer of 200 acres.	Aberdeenshire/ Birse
Elspet Shaw	W	M	42		Banffshire/ Enzie
Elizabeth Ross	D	U	17		Aberdeenshire/ Birse
Mary A. Ross	D	U	15		Aberdeenshire/ Birse
Isabella Ross	D	U	11	Scholar	Aberdeenshire/ Birse
William Ross	S	U	8	Scholar	Aberdeenshire/ Birse
John Smith	Se	U	20	Farm Servant	Aberdeenshire/ Birse
James Shaw *	Se	U	44	Farm Servant	Banffshire/ Enzie
Alexander Brown	Se	U	27	Shepherd/ Farm Servant	Aberdeenshire/ Lumphanen

* James is Elspet's (Elizabeth) brother.

1891 Census, Tillentiach, Birse, Aberdeenshire.

Name	C	S	A	Occupation	Birth Place
James Ross	H	M	70	Farmer	Aberdeenshire/ Birse
Elspet Shaw	W	M	51		Banffshire/ Fordyce
Mary A. Ross	D	U	25		Aberdeenshire/ Birse
Isabel Ross	D	U	21		Aberdeenshire/ Birse
Alexander Grant	Se	U	20	Farm Servant	Kincardine/ Banchory
William Calvin	Se	U	14	Farm Servant	Kincardine/ Durris

James Ross, brothers and sisters, and his parents are also on the 1841, 1851 and 1861 census for Tillenteach Farm, Birse.

Left is a picture of Tillenteach Farm as it stands in 1995.

7.   Mary Ann Shaw, Ref. 194,
      Born - 26/07/1842, Towie Parish, Banffshire
      Occ. - Domestic Servant
      Married - 29/12/1863, Commercial Inn, Keith.
      Spouse - William Wilson, Ref. 218,
           (Son of Alexander Wilson and Jessie Cattell)
      Bap.- 05/02/1836, Drainie, Morayshire
      Occ.- Mason,

      Children:

           i   John Alexander Wilson, Ref. 712,
                   Born - 23/11/1864, St. Nicholas, Aberdeen

           ii   Agnes Wilson, Ref. 713 (See No. 14)
                   Born - 25/10/1866,

           iii   Mary Ann Wilson, Ref. 714,
                   Born - 02/06/1871, 29 Huntly Street, Aberdeen

The census records on the next page are for the Wilson Family.

1881 Census 29 Huntly Street, Aberdeen

Name	C	S	A	Occupation	Birth Place
William Wilson	H	M	44	Stone Cutter	Elginshire, Drainie
Mary A. Wilson	W	M	37		Banffshire, ?
John A. Wilson	S	U	16	Pupil Teacher	Aberdeenshire, OldMachar
Agnes Wilson	D		14	Pupil Teacher	Aberdeen, OldMachar
Mary A. Wilson	D		9	Scholar	Aberdeen, OldMachar

1891 Census 29 Huntly Street, Aberdeen.

Name	C	S	A	Occupation	Birth Place
William Wilson	H	M	54	Stonecutter	Morayshire, Drainie
Mary Ann Wilson	W	M	48		Banffshire, Fordyce
John A. Wilson	S	U	26	Law Clerk	Aberdeenshire, St. Nicholas
Mary A. Wilson	D	U	19		Aberdeenshire, OldMachar

8.   Helen Shaw, Ref. 195,
        Born - 17/06/1844, Towie Parish, Banffshire
        Occ. - Housekeeper
        Married - 10/05/1866, R.C. Church, Keith.
        Spouse - Peter Wright, Ref. 690,
                (Son of James Wright and Margaret Robb)
        Born - 1841 approx,
        Died - 28/12/1878, Perth Infirmary
        Occ. - Railway Porter/Yardsman

Peter's (690) cause of death given on death certificate was that he got accidentally run over by a railway tram. The usual residence was given as 18 Paul Street, Perth.

        Children:
                i   John Wright, Ref. 691,
                        Born - 01/11/1866, Moss Street, Keith.

                ii   William Wright, Ref. 719.
                        Born - 28/12/1868, Perth, Perthshire,

iii   James Alexander George Wright, Ref. 720,
Born - 21/04/1871, Perth, Perthshire,

iv   George Wright, Ref. 721,
Born - 04/11/1873, 18 Paul Street, Perth,

v   Peter Wright, Ref. 722,
Born - 1877 Approx, Perth, Perthshire

Below is the census record of the Wright family 1881.

1881 Census 41 Queen Street, Aberdeen.

Name	C	S	A	Occupation	Birth Place
Hellen Wright	H	W	35		Banffshire, Fordyce
John Wright	S		14	Message Boy	Banffshire, Keith
William Wright	S		12	Message Boy	Perth
George Wright	S		7	Scholar	Perth
Peter Wright	S		4		Perth

9.   George Shaw, Ref. 175,
Born - 15/08/1846, Towie Parish, Banffshire.
Died - 22/01/1928, 62 Union Grove, Aberdeen.
Buried - Alenvale Cemetery, Aberdeen.
Occ. - Shirt, Jacket Manufacturer in Aberdeen.
Married (1) - 14/07/1870 in the RC Church, Huntly St, Aberdeen.
Married (2) - 06/11/1892 in the St Mary's RC Church, Huntly St., Aberdeen.
Spouse (1) - Margaret Tawse, Ref. 176,
          (Daughter of John Tawse & Margaret Davidson)
Born - 1840 Approx, Banchory,
Died - 10/12/1891, Aberdeen,
Buried - Allenvale Cemetery, Aberdeen.
Occ. - Dressmaker
Spouse (2) - Christina Youngson, Ref. 178,
          (Daughter of George Youngson & Christina Wilson)
Born - 24/02/1859, 34 North Broadford, Aberdeen
Died - 31/07/1913, Aberdeen,
Buried - Allenvale Cemetery, Aberdeen,
Occ.- Sewing Machinist.

Children by Margaret Tawes:

    i   Nellie Shaw, Ref. 177,
        Born - 30/06/1881, Aberdeen
        Died - 03/07/1881, 19 Guest Row, Aberdeen.
        Buried - Allenvale Cemetery, Aberdeen.

Children by Christina Youngson:

    ii   John Shaw, Ref. 179,
        Born - 19/08/1893, 62 Union Grove, Aberdeen.
        Died - 25/04/1918, France,
        Occ.- Insurance Clerk.

    iii   Cecilia Shaw, Ref. 180,
        Born - 30/01/1895,
        Died - 07/12/1971,
        Buried - Banchory Ternan Cemetery,
        Occ. - Teacher,

Pictured left is the grave stone in Banchory Ternan Cemetery, where Cecilia Shaw is buried. Also Annie Youngson is buried there, who was a cousin of Cecilia. Her computer Ref. is 397.

Pictured right is the staff of the Summer Street School in Aberdeen. L to R, Mr McGrath, ?, Cissy Shaw, Maggie Fitzpatrick, ?,?.

iv   Josephine Shaw, Ref. 181,
Born - 07/01/1897, 62 Union Grove, Aberdeen.
Died - 03/05/1973,
Occ.- Nun.

v   Robert Shaw, Ref. 182 (See No.15)
Born - 22/12/1898,

vi   George Shaw, Ref. 183 (See No.16)
Born - 22/12/1898,

vii   Alice Adelaide Youngson Shaw, Ref. 184
Born - 11/03/1900, 62 Union Grove, Aberdeen.
Died - 11/01/1941, Royal Infirmary, Aberdeen
Buried - King Street Cemetery

viii   Gwendoline Anna Walpole Shaw, Ref. 155, (See No.17)
Born - 04/04/1902,

These records below show census records for the family of George Shaw and Margaret Tawse.

1871 Census 13 Commerce Street, Aberdeen.

Name	C	S	A	Occupation	Birth Place
George Shaw	H	M	25	Tailor, Clothier	Banffshire/ Fordyce
Margaret Shaw	W	M	30	Tailor's Wife	Kincardineshire/ Banchory

1881 Census 19 Guestrow, Aberdeen.

Name	C	S	A	Occupation	Birth Place
George Shaw	H	M	34	Tailor, Merchant	Banffshire/ Fordyce
Margaret Shaw	W	M	40		Kincardineshire/ Banchory
John Tawse	BL	U	45	Clerk, Cammunical Co	Aberdeenshire/ Birse

1891 Census 62 Union Grove, Aberdeen.

Name	C	S	A	Occupation	Birth Place
George Shaw	H	M	44	Shirt, Jkt Manufacturer	Aberdeenshire/ Fordyce
Margaret Shaw	W	M	?		Aberdeenshire/ Banchory
Mary Watt	Se	U	?	Domestic Ser.	Aberdeenshire/ Chapel of Garioch

Pictured below left is Alice Shaw and below right is a picture of L to R is Alice, Cissy and Gwen Shaw in the garden of 62 Union Grove, Aberdeen.

<u>Notes taken from Aberdeen Directories.</u>

These are to do with his shirt manufacturers company and addresses at which he lived.
H = Home address

<u>1887-88</u>
George Shaw   Shirtmaker
                                     22 Bridge Street.

<u>1888-89</u>
George Shaw   Shirtmaker
                                     8 College Street.

                                     (H) 62 Union Grove.

<u>1889-1901</u>
George Shaw   Shirtmaker
                                     6 College Street.

                                     (H) 62 Union Grove.

<u>1901-05</u>
George Shaw   Shirtmaker
                                     6 College Street.

                                     (H) 48 Stanley Street.

<u>1905-10</u>
George Shaw   Wholesale clothing manufacturer and shirtmaker.
                                     17 St. Nicholas Street.

                                     (H) 48 Stanley Street.

<u>1910-22</u>
George Shaw   Wholesale clothing manufacturer and shirtmaker.
                                     24 Green.

                                     (H) 66 Stanley Street.

<u>1923-24</u>
George Shaw   (H) 66 Stanley Street.

<u>1925-28</u>
George Shaw   (H) 62 Union Grove.

Left Side of Monument.

ERECTED BY
REV. JOHN SHAW C.C.
AND HIS BROTHER
GEORGE
IN LOVING MEMORY OF
THEIR FATHER
JOHN SHAW MILLER
WHO DIED 29 NOV 1883
AGE 89 YEARS
ALSO OF HIS WIFE
MARY GREEN
THEIR MOTHER
WHO DIED 27 SEP 1887
AGE 84 YEARS
JOHN SHAW
SON OF THE SAID GEORGE SHAW
FELL IN ACTION IN FRANCE
25 APRIL 1918
AGE 25 YEARS
R.I.P.

Front of Monument.

IN LOVING MEMORY OF
MARGARET TAWSE
WIFE OF
GEORGE SHAW
MANUFACTURER ABERDEEN
WHO DIED 10 DEC 1891
AGE 51 YEARS
AND OF THEIR INFANT DAUGHTER
NELLIE
WHO DIED 3 JULY 1881
AGE 3 DAYS
ALSO OF
CHRISTINA YOUNGSON
WIFE OF THE SAID GEORGE SHAW
WHO DIED 31 JULY 1913
AGE 55 YEARS
AND THE SAID GEORGE SHAW
WHO DIED 22 JAN 1928
AGE 81 YEARS
R.I.P

13 Commerse Street, Aberdeen
The picture right taken in April 1994 shows the area in which 13 Commerse Street stood in the 1870's when George stayed there.

Guest Row, Aberdeen
Pictured left taken in April 1994 is of Provost Skenes House which is the last building left still standing from Guestrow where George lived in the 1880's.
Provost Skenes House is now a museum and coffee house which is visited by many holiday makers every year.

22 Bridge Street, Aberdeen.
George had his manufacturing buisness in this building in the upper part of building between 1887 and 1888.
This picture right was taken in October 1993.

6 & 8 College Street, Aberdeen.

George had his manufacturing business in 8 College Street between 1888 and 1889 then during 1889 moved to 6 staying till 1905.

The picture right taken in October 1993 shows the area that the above premises stood.

17 St. Nicholas Street, Aberdeen.

George had his manufacturing business in these premises between 1905 and 1910.

The area where 17 was, now has the St. Nicholas Centre on it which is pictured below left taken in October 1993. Also below right is a postcard of St Nicholas Street in the late 1880's.

24 The Green, Aberdeen

George had his manufacturing business in this premises between 1910 and 1912. The picture right taken in October 1993 shows the area 24 The Green would have been.

62 Union Grove, Aberdeen.

George lived in 62 Union Grove at different time during his life owning it during his later stays.

The periods of stay were -

1888 - 1901
1925 - 1930

Pictured right 62 Union Grove as it stands in October 1993.

48 Stanley Street, Aberdeen.

George lived at 48 Stanley Street from 1901 to 1910 which is pictured left as it stands in October 1993.

<u>66 Stanley Street, Aberdeen.</u>

George lived at 66 Stanley Street between 1910 and 1924 which is pictured right as it stands in October 1993.

10.   Catherine Sim, Ref. 1143,
       Born - 1847/48 Approx, Old Machar Parish, Aberdeenshire
       Occ.- Domestic Servant,
       Married - 13/06/1880, 57 Queen Street, Aberdeen,
       Spouse - John Jack, Ref. 1137,
                (Son of William Jack and Mary Smith)
       Born - 27/02/1841, Old Meldrum Parish, Aberdeenshire,
       Occ.- Stoneware Merchant,

       Children:
                i   Margaret Shaw Jack, Ref. 1144
                         Born - 19/07/1880, 57 Queen Street, Aberdeen,

                ii   Lizzie Jack, Ref. 1181
                         Born - 1882, Aberdeen,

                iii   Thomas Watson Jack, Ref. 1145
                         Born - 11/12/1883, 69 Queen Street, Aberdeen,

                iv   Catherine Jack, Ref. 1182
                         Born - 1888, Aberdeen,

31

v   Henry Jack, Ref. 1183
Born - 1890, Aberdeen

John Jack was a widower with 3 children when he married Catherine. The children's names were Jane, George and John.

1881 Census 57 Queen Street, Aberdeen

Name	C	S	A	Occupation	Birth Place
John Jack	H	M	39	Stoneware Merchant	Old Meldrum, Aberdeenshire
Catherine Jack	W	M	32		Old Machar, Aberdeenshire
Jane Jack	D	U	15	Stoneware Merchant	Inverurie, Aberdeenshire
George Jack	S	U	9	Scholar	St Nicholas, Aberdeenshire
John Jack	S	U	7	Scholar	St Nicholas, Aberdeenshire
Margaret Jack	D		8m		St Nicholas, Aberdeenshire

1891 Census 26 1/2 Roslin Terrace, Aberdeen

Name	C	S	A	Occupation	Birth Place
John Jack	H	M	48	Warehouse Porter	Old Meldrum, Aberdeenshire
Catherine Jack	W	M	42		Old Machar, Aberdeenshire
John Jack	S		17	House Painter	Aberdeen
Margaret Jack	D		10		Aberdeen
Lizzie Jack	D		9		Aberdeen
Thomas Jack	S		7		Aberdeen
Catherine Jack	D		3		Aberdeen
Henry Jack	S		1		Aberdeen

FOURTH GENERATION

11.   John Strachan, Ref. 738,
       Born - 10/06/1859, Craigmills, Fordyce, Banffshire
       Occ.- Farmer
       Married - 11/08/1887, Pairhead or Parkhead, King Edward, Aberdeenshire,
       Spouse - Annie Morrison, Ref. 742,
                (Daughter of John Morrison & Elizabeth Duncan)
       Born - 1864 Approx,

       Children:
                i   Mary A. Strachan, Ref. 751
                       Born - 1889 Approx, King Edward, Aberdeenshire

                ii   Elsie M. Strachan, Ref. 752,
                       Born - 1890 Approx, King Edward, Aberdeenshire

Below is a census report for 1891 for the above family.

1891 Census Morlass Cottage, King Edward, Aberdeenshire.

Name	C	S	A	Occupation	Birth Place
John Strachan	H	M	31	Farmers Son	Fordyce, Banffshire
Anne Strachan	W	M	28	Farmers Wife	King Edward, Aberdeenshire
Mary A. Strachan	D		2		King Edward, Aberdeenshire
Elsie M. Strachan	D		8m		King Edward, Aberdeenshire

12.   Isabella Ross, Ref. 647,
       Born - 03/05/1869, Tillinteach, Birse,
       Married - 24/08/1894, Tillentech, Birse,
       Spouse - James Laing Webster, Ref. 649,
                (Son of Alexander Webster & Mary Gill)
       Born - 1871 Approx
       Occ.- Ploughman

       Children:
                i   William Alexander Webster, Ref. 650,
                       Born - 03/07/1895, Bellthangie Cottage, Birse

                ii   James Gordon Webster, Ref. 651,
                       Born - 03/11/1899, Tillanteach, Birse

13.   William Ross, Ref. 219,
        Born - 26/11/1872, Tillinteach, Birse
        Occ.- Solicitor, Golden Square, Aberdeen
        Married - 02/09/1902, Grand Hotel, Union Terrace, Aberdeen
        Spouse - Isabella Russell Greig, Ref. 652,
                (Daughter of Alexander Greig & Margaret Simpson)
        Born - 1872 Approx,

        Children:
                i   Isobel Margaret Ross, Ref. 220,
                        Born - 11/08/1905, Forest Avenue, Aberdeen,
                        Spouse - Farquhar McRichie, Ref. 222,

Extract from The Aberdeen Daily Journal   - Births

12/08/1905
ROSS - At 157 Forest Avenue, Aberdeen on the 11 August the wife of William Ross solicitor of a daughter.

The record below is a Census record for William before he was married.

1891 Census 12 Margaret Street, Aberdeen.

Name	C	S	A	Occupation	Birth Place
Elizabeth Ross	H	U	61	Lodging House Keeper	Aberdeenshire, Birse
William Ross	Bo	U	18	Advocates Clerk (Apprentice)	Aberdeenshire, Birse

Extract from Aberdeen Daily Journal - Marriages

03/09/1902
ROSS - GREIG - At the Grand Hotel, Aberdeen on the 2 September by the Rev. C.H.Todd MA of the UF East Church William Ross Solicitor of Aberdeen to Isabella Russell, daughter of Alexander Greig of 17 Osborne Place, Aberdeen.

14.   Agnes Wilson, Ref.713,
        Born - 25/10/1866, OldMachar, Aberdeen
        Occ.- School Teacher
        Married - 08/12/1887, St. Mary's Cathedral, Huntly Street, Aberdeen.
        Spouse - Robert Chisholm Robertson, Ref. 715,
                (Son of Robert Chisolm Robertson & Jane Cotter)
        Born - 1861 Approx
        Occ.- Mining Engineer,

Children:

          i   Moira Robertson, Ref.716 (See No.18)

15.   Robert Shaw, Ref. 182,
        Born - 22/12/1898, 62 Union Grove, Aberdeen
        Died - 22/07/1981,
        Occ.- Banker in Cuba.
        Spouse - Helen, Ref. 223,
        Died - 13/01/1978,
        Occ.- Secretary.

Pictured right is Robert Shaw in Cuba.

Children:

          i   Robert John Shaw, Ref. 224,
                     Born - 1938,

Pictured right is Robert John Shaw, 14 months old, Banes, Oriente, Cuba.

                ii   Betty Shaw, Ref. 225 (See No.19)
                          Born - 1944,

16.   George Shaw, Ref. 183,
        Born - 22/12/1898, 62 Union Grove, Aberdeen
        Died - 29/07/1966,
        Buried - Banchory Ternan Cemetery,
        Occ.- Postman,
        Spouse - May Watt, Ref. 229,
        Died - 31/01/1994, Dundee,
        Service - Monifieth Church, Dundee,
        Buried - 04/02/1994 Banchory Ternan Cemetery,
        Occ.- Shop Owner in Banchory,

        Children:
                i   Josephine Shaw, Ref. 230 (See No. 20)

When George retired as a postman they moved to Banchory and his wife May owned and ran a Ladies clothing shop called May's.

Pictured below is George and May's gravestone in Banchory Ternan Cemetery.

17.   Gwendoline Anna Walpole Shaw, Ref. 155,
        Born - 04/04/1902, 48 Stanley Street, Aberdeen,
        Died - 11/10/1989, Dunblane,
        Buried - Dunblane Cemetery,
        Occ.- Teacher,
        Married - 17/12/1938 in Stirling,
        Spouse - Hugh Smiley, Ref. 154,
                (Son of Alexander Smiley and Mary Caldwell.)
        Born - 14/01/1914, Larne, Northern Ireland,
        Occ.- Electrical Engineer

        Children:
                i   Mary Ann Smiley, Ref. 158,
                        Born - 18/11/1940, Stirling,
                        Died - 08/12/1940, Stirling,
                        Buried - Mar Place, Stirling.

                ii   John Smiley, Ref. 157 (See No.21),
                        Born - 17/10/1941,

                iii   Gwendoline Smiley, Ref. 156 (See No.22),
                        Born - 11/05/1943,

                iv   Margaret Smiley, Ref. 150 (See No.23),
                        Born - 05/07/1945,

Pictured below left is Gwen Shaw and below right is the Gravestone of Gwen Shaw in Dunblane
Cemetery.

37

FIFTH GENERATION

18.   Moira Robertson, Ref. 716,
       Spouse - Mr. McCormick, Ref. 717,

       Children:
                     i   Edward McCormack, Ref. 718,

19.   Betty Shaw, Ref. 225,
       Born - 1944,
       Spouse - Philip LeRoy, Ref. 226,

       Children:
                     i   Sean LeRoy, Ref. 227, (See No. 24)
                              Born - 08/09/1968

                     ii   Yvonne, LeRoy, Ref. 228, (See No. 25)
                              Born -01/06/1974 adpt.,

20.   Josephine Shaw, Ref. 230,
       Born - 12/07/1947, Aberdeen
       Occ - Teacher
       Married - 28/09/1973, Blairs College, Aberdeen,
       Spouse - Len Moir, Ref. 231,

       Children:
                     i   Robbie Moir, Ref. 232,
                              Born- 08/06/1975, Dundee

                     ii   Lucy Moir, Ref. 233,
                              Born- 14/07/1977, Dundee

                     iii   Hamish Moir, Ref.234,
                              Born- 07/12/1980, Dundee

21.   John Smiley Bsc. Dip.Eng. Msc., Ref. 157,
       Born - 17/10/1941,
       Occ.- Electrical Engineer,
       Married - 30/09/1968,
       Spouse - Anita Coletti MA. DIPSE., Ref. 235,
       Born - 09/01/1946,
       Occ.- Teacher,

Children:

i Philip Gregory Smiley BA., Ref. 236,
    Born - 10/09/1969, Stirling Royal Infirmary
    Married - 07/09/1996, St Francis Church, Chester
    Spouse - Yvonne Turley, Ref. 1112
       (Daughter of Brian & Barbara Turley)

ii Dr. Elita Smiley MB ChB, Ref. 237, (See No. 26)
    Born - 09/12/1970,

iii Nicholas Smiley, Ref. 238,
    Born - 29/01/1972,
    Married - 11/07/1997, St Patricks Church, Huddersfield
    Spouse - Christina Lundy, Ref. 1173,
       (Daughter of Patrick Lundy & Mrs Lundy)

iv Laura Smiley, Ref. 239,
    Born - 07/03/1974,

          v   Alexander Hugh Smiley, Ref. 240,
                  Born - 03/11/1980, Aberdeen Royal Infirmary,

          vi   Simon Peter Smiley, Ref. 241,
                  Born - 03/11/1980, Aberdeen Royal Infirmary,

22.   Gwendoline Smiley, Ref. 156,
          Born - 11/05/1943,
          Occ.- Teacher in Winnipeg,
          Married - 08/05/1965,
          Spouse - Dr. Gerald Iliffe, Ref. 242,
          Born - 03/01/1943,

Pictured below is Gwendoline Smiley (156) in Farriers, Alva at Fiona and Euan Bowie's graduation party during July 1994, while she was over from Canada on holiday staying with her father in Dunblane.

Children:

i   Melanie Iliffe, Ref. 243 (See No.27),
           Born - 18/11/1966,

ii   Capt. Roger Iliffe, Ref. 244,
           Born - 19/08/1968, Airthrey Castle, Stirling
           Occ.- Canadian Army,
           Married - 13/08/1997, Budapest, Hungary
           Spouse - Ildiko Maczko, Ref. 1172,
           Born - Hungary

Pictured below is Roger when he visited David and Maggie Bowie during Christmas 1995.

iii   Tracey Jane Iliffe, Ref. 245,
           Born - 29/07/1969,

iv   Emma Rose Iliffe Bsc., Ref. 246,
Born - 14/06/1971,
Married - 12/09/98, Winnipeg, Canada
Spouse - Robert Lee, Ref. 1293,

23.   Margaret Smiley, Ref. 150,
Born - 05/07/1945, 62 Union Grove, Aberdeen,
Married - 04/02/1967, in Dunblane RC Church,
Spouse - David Bowie, Ref. 147,
      (Son of David Bowie and Helen Burt Ferguson.)
Born - 13/02/1942, 42 Primrose Street, Alloa,
Occ.- Trading Standards Officer,.

Picture right is of David and Maggie Bowie going to their son David's Wedding 23/10/1993.

Children:
i   David Alan Bowie B.Eng., Ref. 151,
Born - 06/09/1969, Airthrey Castle, Stirling,
Educated - Alloa Academy,
      Dundee University.

42

Occ.- Civil Engineer
Married - 23/10/1993, in University Chapel, University of Glasgow.
Spouse - Dr. Laura Dunlop Bsc. Phd., Ref. 153,
Born - 02/02/1970, Thailand,

Photo right is of Airthrey Castle (Taken from the top of Wallace Monument) where David was born.

Pictured right are David and Laura at their wedding reception at Glasgow University 23/10/1993.

43

ii   Dr. Fiona Margaret Bowie MB ChB, Ref. 2,
Born - 15/03/1971, Stirling Maternity Home,
Occ.- Medical Doctor,
Married - 01/08/1992, in St. Mungo's R.C. Church, Alloa, by
      Father James Hunter High.
Spouse - Charles Gordon Seaman, Ref. 1,
      (Son of Charles Donald McDonald Seaman and Winifred
      Margareta Mackenzie.)
Born - 05/04/1961, Simpson Memorial Maternity Pavillion
      Edinburgh.
Educated - Lochaber High School,
Occ.- Welder, Sports Shop Manager, Leisure Attendant.

Photo on right is of Charlie and Fiona in 1991.

iii   Euan Alistair Bowie B.Eng., Ref. 152,
Born - 01/06/1972, Stirling Royal Infirmary,
Occ.- Civil Engineer,

On the next page is a picture of Euan after his graduation at Dundee Uni. in 1994.

SIXTH GENERATION

24.   Sean Leroy, Ref. 227,
       Spouse - Rebecca, Ref. 1289,

       Children:
                  i   Megan Ann LeRoy, Ref. 1290,
                           Born - June 1996,

25.   Yvonne Leroy, Ref. 228,
       Married - March 97,
       Spouse - Mr Lee, Ref. 1291,

       Children:
                  i   Philip Lee, Ref. 1292,
                           Born - August 97,

26.   Dr. Elita Smiley MB ChB, Ref. 237,
        Born - 09/12/1970,
        Occ.- Medical Doctor
        Married - 28/07/1995, University of Glasgow Chapel, Glasgow.
        Spouse - Mark Storey, Ref. 827,

        Children:
                    i   Peter John Storey, Ref. 1120,
                            Born - 12/08/1996, Paisley

                    ii   Michael Storey, Ref. 1294,
                            Born - 26/01/1998, Paisley

Picture right is of Elita Smiley's
wedding.

27.   Melanie Iliffe, Ref. 243,
        Born - 18/11/1966,
        Married - 14/02/1992, Winnipeg, Canada,
        Occ.- Radiographer,
        Spouse - Adam Nitychoruk, Ref. 255,
        Occ.- Mechanical Engineer

        Children:
                    i   Amanda Ruth Nitychoruk, Ref. 256,
                            Born - 10/10/1991,

                    ii   Joseph Marion Nitychoruk, Ref. 257,
                            Born - 14/06/1993,

                    iii   Luke Nitychoruk, Ref. 1180,
                            Born - 01/02/1997,